Financial Markets and Services

FINANCIAL MARKETS AND SERVICES

DR. P. BALAJI
SURBHI BIRLA
PRANJAL RAWAT
DR. M. JAYALAKSHMI
DR. K. SUMITHA

INDIA

FINANCIAL MARKETS AND SERVICES

by: Dr. P. Balaji, Surbhi Birla, Pranjal Rawat, Dr. M. Jayalakshmi, Dr. K. Sumitha

■

RED'SHINE PUBLICATION PVT. LTD.
Headquarters (India): 88-90 REDMAC, Navamuvada,
Lunawada, India-389 230
Contact: +91 76988 26988
Registration no. GJ31D0000034

In Association with,
RED'MAC INTERNATIONAL PRESS & MEDIA. INC
India | Sweden | UK

■

■

■

ISBN: 978-93-93239-00-6
ISBN-10: 93-93239-00-2
DIP: 18.10.9393239002
DOI: 10.25215/9393239002
Price: ₹ 400
April, 2022 (First Edition)

■

■

www.redshine.co.in | info@redshine.in
Printed in India | Title ID: 9393239002

CONTENTS

UNIT-I
FINANCIAL SYSTEM

A well-functioning economy relies heavily on a well-developed financial system. In order for an economy to grow, it needs to have a strong financial system.

One of the most critical elements in the growth of our country's economy is the Indian Financial System. Investors and businesses benefit from this system by channelling money from the country's citizens (household savings) to those who can make intelligent use of it (investors/businessmen).

Aspirants preparing for various government exams in the country should take the time to read this article thoroughly and make the necessary preparations.

The financial system serves as a means of exchanging goods and services by facilitating the payment of invoices. Investors and savers are connected by this service.

DEFINITION OF FINANCIAL SYSTEM

Net savers can lend money to net spenders through the financial system. To ensure that funds are transferred and investment is maintained in the economy.

"Financial institutions, markets, and securities are all components of the financial system," according to this definition.

STRUCTURE OF INDIAN FINANCIAL SYSTEM.

FINANCIAL INSTITUTIONS

Financial institutions serve as mediators between investors and borrowers, ensuring the proper operation of the financial system. They use the surplus units' savings to fund productive activities with a higher rate of return on investment. Companies that need to raise money can rely on them for a wide range of services. For a financial system to work properly, financial institutions are critical.

An intermediary between the investor and borrower is provided by Financial Institutions. The Financial Markets are used to either directly or indirectly mobilise an investor's savings.

FUNCTIONS OF THE FINANCIAL INSTITUTIONS

A short-term obligation can be transformed into a long-term asset.

A dangerous investment can be converted into an investment that is risk-free with this tool.

Additionally, it is used to match small deposits with large loans and large deposits with smaller loans.

A bank is an excellent illustration of a financial institution. People who have extra cash set it aside in savings accounts, while others who are strapped for cash turn to loans.

FINANCIAL INSTITUTIONS

Banking Institutions or Depository Institutions – Those institutions include banks and other credit unions that gather money from the general population and lend it to that in need at interest.

• **Non-Banking Institutions or Non-Depository Institutions** This group includes businesses including insurance companies, mutual funds, and brokerage firms. However, they are prohibited from requesting monetary deposits from their customers.

FINANCIAL ASSETS

This is an essential part of the financial system. monetary contracts are the basis of financial instruments. Financial assets, securities, and other sorts of financial instruments are all traded on the financial market. Because the needs of investors and credit seekers are different, there are a wide variety of securities available in the market.

Financial Assets

Call Money – One-day loans are known as "call money" since they must be repaid the next day. This type of transaction does not necessitate the use of any type of collateral.

Notice Money – The term "notice money" refers to money borrowed for a period longer than a day but shorter than 14 days. This type of transaction does not necessitate the use of any type of collateral.

Term Money – Term money is money that has a maturity time of more than 14 days.

Treasury Bills – Treasury bills have a maturity of less than a year and are therefore referred to as T-Bills. When you buy a T-Bill, you're effectively lending the government money.

Certificate of Deposits – Money put in a bank for a set period of time takes on a digital form (is generated electronically).

Commercial Paper – It is a short-term, unsecured debt instrument issued by corporations.

FINANCIAL SERVICES

Asset and Liability Management firms provide the services that make up this industry. They assist in raising the necessary finances and ensure that they are put to good use. Professional services are extended up to the point of servicing lenders by these consultants.

The Indian financial system's structure is made up with A financial system is one that facilitates the transfer of money from one party to another. At both the national and global levels, the Indian financial systems are active. They're made up of a slew of interconnected marketplaces, services, and organisations whose sole purpose is to connect investors with depositors on a daily basis.

Financial services:

- **Banking Services** – Depositing money, issuing debit/credit cards, creating accounts and more are all examples of banking services.

- **Insurance Services-** Insurance services include everything from issuing and selling insurance policies to insurance undertakings and brokerages.
- **Investment Services** – It mostly entails the management of assets.

There are many financial services out there, but their primary function is to aid people in selling or borrowing securities and making payments, as well as facilitating lending and investing.

FINANCIAL MARKETS

Lender-to-borrower negotiations, such as those that take place between a small business owner who is borrowing from a bank or a small loan firm, are common in financial markets. The open loan market is another type of negotiation. A market where conventional securities are traded in enormous amounts, on the other hand, is a cold, impersonal one. An open market is something like the stock exchange. As a general rule, the financial markets are credit markets that serve to the needs of individuals, organisations, and networks. Credit is given on both a short and long term basis.

When buyers and sellers come together in a financial market, they trade money, bonds and other financial instruments.

CLASSIFICATION OF FINANCIAL MARKET

Money Market

The financial market includes the money market. Trading in short-term debt investments from one to 90 days is referred to as the money market. RBI is in charge of overseeing it (reserve bank of India). This is the wholesale market, and the amount of transactions here is significant.

When it comes to short-term investments, the money market is where you'll find them exchanged. To enable short-term financing and to ensure the liquidity of short-term financial assets, the money market exists. The surpluses and short-term cash deficits can be met by using this medium. As a result, anyone who has a surplus of investable funds can use the money market to store and earn a return on those funds for a limited time. Individuals, organisations, and governments who are experiencing a short-term liquidity crunch can borrow money on the money market. As a result of the money market, borrowers and lenders alike may rest easy knowing that they can get their hands on short-term funds when they need them. Most of the central bank's operations are conducted on the money market, where it regulates and controls the economy's money supply. The money market reduces default and loss of capital risk to a minimum. As a result of the short-term nature of money market products, there is minimal money risk. The role of the central bank in the money market is critical. It is revered as the 'presiding deity' of the financial markets, and for good reason. It is not only a watchdog of the monetary system, but also a promoter and developer of economic growth. The central bank regulates money and credit supply in a country by quantitative and qualitative methods such as the bank rate, open market operations, the reserves ratio, margin restrictions, moral suasion, and consumer credit regulation.

Instrument in Money Market

Treasury Bills: These are financial assets that can be traded. The Reserve Bank of India (RBI) issues it. Three different lengths of time can be used for the issuing of T-bills: 91 days, 182 days, and 364. It is up to the market to establish the interest rate on T-bills.

Call Money: An extremely short-term loan known as a "call" is a form of call money. It's only good for one day, after all. When a sudden influx of cash is needed, this is what you need.

Certificate of Deposit: When it comes to saving, a Certificate of Deposit (CD) is the best option. A negotiable financial instrument that is not secured by any collateral. Institutions, people, corporations, trusts, and funds can all receive certificates from it. It ranges from a few days to a few months.

Commercial Bills: A legitimate business transaction results in a commercial bill of exchange. High liquidity and minimal risk make it a good investment option. It ranges from a few days to a few months.

Capital Market

A financial market where long-term investments such as stocks, bonds, and other types of debt are traded is known as a capital market. It focuses on long-term and medium-term investments. It is overseen by the (SEBI) .

In a capital market, lenders or investors trade long-term cash for financial assets from borrowers or holders in exchange for those assets. Directing money into long-term investments is the key goal for capital markets (mostly for a period of one year and above). Markets for money and capital are distinguished by the varying maturities of their financial assets. Although the one-year dividing line between the money and the capital markets is arbitrary, it is widely accepted. Individuals, institutions, the federal and state governments, local self-governments, and private corporations all have a need for long-term funding. The new issue market consists of shares, debentures, and bonds, all of which are sold to raise money. Debt-financed deficit units also rely on long-term capital from public financial institutions and investment firms. Individuals (households), institutions, banks, and industrial financial institutions are the primary sources of funding. The financial system relies heavily on the capital markets. The development and expansion of an economy depends on the ability of people to save and invest. Capital markets serve as a conduit via which surplus units' savings can be converted into long-term investments by deficit units. In addition to other factors, the rate of long-term investment and capital formation in a country determines the pace of economic development. Savings, investment, and financial markets all influence capital production. Savings are mobilised and made available to savvy investors thanks in large part to the stock market. The secondary market serves as a source of liquidity for the current stock market. Incentives and punishments are used to distribute monies in the system. Due to the lower risk of their securities, large and well-established enterprises typically have lower capital costs. Investing in high-growth companies can fetch a premium on the market, but investing in low-growth companies can be difficult, and the latter may have to issue shares at a discount in order to obtain more money. No matter how you slice it, non-specified stock is far more appealing than specified stock.

Primary Markets: Investing in long-term securities on the open market is known as the primary market. This market has a fixed pricing.

Secondary Markets: To describe a market in which issued securities are traded, the term "secondary market" has been coined. Prices are set by the dynamics of supply and demand in this market.

Instrument Trade In Capital Market :

Non-Security Market

- **Mutual Funds**: When it comes to mutual funds, you'll find a wide range of investments from equities to bonds, as well as short and long term investment options. To limit risk, a fund manager gathers money from a large number of investors and invests it in a variety of financial assets.
- **Bank Deposits**: You have a bank deposit if you have money in a bank account. Depending on the institution, it could be in a savings or a fixed-term investment account.
- **Provident Funds**: In the event of an employee's death, he or she will get the full amount he or she contributed to the Provident Funds with interest.
- **Small Savings**: It's termed personal savings when you set aside a portion of your earnings for the future. We set aside funds in case of unforeseen circumstances or the desire to acquire financial assets.

Security Market

- **Share**: Long-term financing comes in the form of stock in any company. In the secondary market, it can be bought and sold.

The corporation never returns any of its money. Equity shares and Preference shares are the two types of shares.

- **Debentures**: As a debt instrument, debentures are issued by a firm for the purpose of raising capital. A debenture is often unsecured and long-term in nature.

FINANCIAL INSTRUMENTS

Claims on assets that are represented by financial instruments are known as "financial instruments." As previously stated, a financial asset is a claim to the repayment of a specific amount of money, plus interest or dividend, at the conclusion of a specified term. Promissory Note, Treasury Bill, Government Bond, Deposit Receipt, Share, and Debenture are all examples of bills of exchange.

Financial securities are also known as financial instruments. Classifications of financial securities include

Primary securities

Shares and debentures issued to the public directly by the final investors are examples of these instruments.

Secondary securities

Investors buy these securities from financial intermediaries, such as the Unit Trust of India and Mutual Funds, who issue them in the form of units and then pool the resulting funds to invest in businesses.

These securities can also be categorised according to their length of time, as follows:

1. Short-term financial instruments.

(iii) Short-term investments.

Third: long-term investments.

There are a number of short-term securities, including the bill of exchange, the Treasury bill and so on. Debentures with five-year duration are considered medium-term securities since they have an expiration date of one to five years. To qualify as long-term securities, an investment must have a maturity length of at least five years, such as ten-year government bonds.

Features of financial instruments

With a few simple man oeuvres, most instruments may be swapped from one hand to another.

It is possible to trade in these securities because they have a ready market, which means that they can be traded on a regular basis.

(iii) They have a high degree of liquidity, which means that some instruments can be easily exchanged for cash. Discounting and rediscounting a bill of exchange, for example, is a simple way to turn it into cash.

In most cases, securities can be used as collateral to raise loans.

When it comes to the payment of principle, interest, or dividends, there is a degree of ambiguity.

These instruments make it easier to trade futures contracts to protect against the risks associated with price and interest rate volatility.

In general, the costs of buying and selling these assets are lower than those of other types of investments.

These instruments' returns are inversely proportional to the degree of uncertainty they entail.

FINANCIAL INTERMEDIARIES

There are many different types of financial intermediaries, including money market intermediates for individuals and businesses. All types of financial institutions and investment institutions are included in this definition, which encompasses all types of financial transactions.

They can work in either a structured or unstructured environment.

Capital market intermediaries

Individuals and corporations are the primary customers of these intermediaries, which primarily offer long-term financing. These institutions include both short-term lenders like banks and long-term investors like the Investment Company of India (LIC).

Money market intermediaries

Only short-term funds are available to customers of money market intermediaries.

FINANCIAL INSTITUTIONS

Financial institutions are organisations that provide their customers or members with financial services. Financial intermediation is the most likely service. Banks, trusts and corporations are only few of the institutions that fall under the umbrella of financial institutions.

Investment, loans, and deposits are only a few examples of the types of financial transactions handled by a financial institution. Financial institutions can be for-profit or not-for-profit organisations that collect money from customers and invest it in a number of ways that benefit both the customer and the business as a whole.

Feature of Financial Institutions:

- It's both a building block and a go-between.
- It transforms a person's savings into an investment.
- These financial assets include the likes of deposits, borrowings, and other forms of borrowing security.
- Non-banking institutions are also included.
- It encompasses both formal and informal organisations.
- Initiated with a clearly defined purpose.
- Governed and regulated by a higher authority.
- Deposits can be made.
- It lends money for business, residential, and commercial real estate purposes.

CLASSIFICATION OF FINANCIAL INSTITUTIONS:

Banking Institutions

Deposits from the general public are accepted, and the money is then loaned to those in need. These are primarily set up to make money, but they also serve to protect the interests of the members. It is the responsibility of banks to make sure that the money customers deposit is put to good use.

A) Commercial banks: These institutions are also known as commercial banks.

Commercial banks fall into one of the following categories. i. The general public. II. The private sector. a) Banks in small towns and rural areas third-party banks

B) Cooperative Banks: Its members' interests are protected by these measures. Cooperatively run, they take deposits and provide loans to their members.

Non-banking Institutions

Banks that don't satisfy the legal definition of a bank provide banking services anyway. There are other non-banking financial institutions that collect money from the public either directly or indirectly. They lend the funds that have been gathered together. Organizational and non-organizational non-banking institutions are divided into two categories:

Non-banking institutions include the following: Provisional and pension funds, for example. iii. A small-scale savings group. ' Life Insurance Company of America (LIC). fourth-generation general insurance company (GIC). indian trust company unit trust v. (UTI). It's a mutual fund! Investment trusts, for example.

Importance of Financial Institutions:

Economic activity relies heavily on the funding provided by financial institutions. Many benefits flow from a country's financial institutions being solid and healthy. FI's significance can be summarised as follows:

Provide funds: Investment and industrial activity are funded by financial institutions.

Infrastructural facilities: For the establishment and promotion of profitable companies, financial institutions also provide fundamental infrastructure facilities. Development of industrial estates, tech parks, roads, and waterways are all examples of infrastructure.

Promotional activities: Financial institutions engage in promotional efforts in order to raise cash, decrease the risk of selling financial assets, and arrange the working and long-term capital of the firm.

Development of backward areas: As a part of their social responsibility, financial institutions give free loans, free education, and job development to those living in economically depressed areas. **Planned development**: All planned developments are initiated by financial institutions with the goal of promoting economic growth in the state. Government and social welfare are incorporated into all future development projects.

Accelerating industrialization: Because financial organisations exist to make money and protect their members' interests, they contribute to industrial expansion through promoting industrialization. They help businesses by providing financing, project development, and consulting services.

Functions of Financial Institutions

Primary functions: Banks and other financial organisations, such as co-operative societies and insurance companies, perform these core functions. These are the primary purposes of the device:

Accepting deposits: Deposits from the general public are accepted by the majority of financial institutions, including commercial banks and cooperative societies. Customers can choose from a variety of ways to raise funds from the public. Interest is paid on accepted deposits by financial institutions based on the length of the deposit term.

Providing Real estate loans: As well as loans and advances for the purchase and building of commercial and residential property, financial institutions also assist the real estate industry.

Providing mortgage loans: Financial institutions also lend money to those who need it, based on collateral such as property and other assets. For example, a gold loan, a property loan, or any other type of loan where the collateral is gold or property.

Issuing share certificates: Securities issued by established corporations to their shareholders are likewise handled by financial institutions. Shares investment funds are also accepted from investors, and the corporations are authorised to issue certificates on behalf of the investors.

Secondary Functions: In addition to the aforementioned basic duties, financial institutions also execute the following secondary responsibilities. The following is a list of secondary functions:

Act as an intermediary: As a bridge between the savings community and the industrialist, financial institutions serve as intermediaries. Their interest rate on the public deposit is far lower than their interest rate on lending the same money to the needy group. As a result of their middleman services, they earn a profit on the interest rate differential.

FINANCIAL SERVICE

The term "financial service" refers to financial services provided by financial institutions to their customers. Its goal is to function as a go-between for private investors as well as large institutions in their financial dealings. Financial intermediation is another name for financial services. Financial intermediation is the process of utilising human surplus and distributing the resulting funds to a variety of organisations in need (such as industries, businesses, individuals, and so on) in order to spur economic growth.

Individuals and organisations alike rely on financial services for advice and assistance in a wide range of areas, including personal finances, leasing, investment management and insurance. For the creation of new businesses, the expansion of existing industries, and the growth of the economy, financial services are critical. When it comes to financial markets, financial services can help with everything from borrowing and selling securities to lending and investing, as well as processing payments and settlements and managing risk exposures. In the leasing industry, mutual funds are a popular choice. In the merchant banking industry, portfolio managers and bill discounting and acceptance businesses are also popular choices. They need a variety of financial services to be able to perform the assigned tasks. Because of this, financial services are a part of the financial system.

IMPORTANT TYPES OF FINANCIAL SERVICES:

BANKING SERVICES:

- Banks' fundamental functions are to keep money safe while allowing customers to withdraw it when necessary.
- Cheque books are given out to customers.
- Loans for personal use, business purposes, and home purchases are all available.
- Issuance of credit cards, as well as the processing and billing of credit card purchases.
- issuing debit cards in place of paper checks.
- Branches and ATMs should be able to process financial transactions (ATMs)
- E-transfers of funds between financial institutions
- Payments can be made automatically via standing orders and direct debits.
- Establish overdraft agreements.
- Financial and other documents can be notarized.
- To help people with their financial and tax planning needs.

Foreign Exchange Services

Many banks throughout the world offer foreign exchange services. Included in our foreign currency services:

Investment Services: The phrase "asset management" is commonly used to describe organisations that manage mutual funds. Primary brokerage units at large investment banks are commonly used by hedge funds to carry out their trades.

Custody Services: For financial services, "back-office" notes management is provided by custodial services and securities processing.

Insurance Services: Insurers, brokers, underwriters, and reinsurers are all included in its scope.

Other Financial Services Stock brokers (private client services) and discount brokers are involved in these activities. Traders use stock brokers to buy or sell shares.

Private Equity: Typically, closed-end private equity funds invest in businesses that are either privately held or will be taken private after an acquisition. It is possible for the most successful private equity funds to outperform the stock market in terms of returns.

CLASSIFICATION OF FINANCIAL SERVICES

Fund Based Services: Financial services that are provided on a commission or interest basis are known as fund-based or asset-based financial services.

Leasing: 'Lease' refers to an agreement between a landlord and a tenant to use a property for a predetermined length of time in exchange for a monthly or annual fee.

Factoring: It is a service offered by a factor (financial institution) to its clients (companies) in which the factor buys the clients' debts and receivable accounts at discount rates and provides instant cash. Factoring is a term for this service. This type of financing is often referred to as account receivables finance.

Bills Discounting: Discounting a bill of exchange is trading or selling a bill to a financial institution prior to its maturity time for a discount rate. The discount rate is determined by the remaining time before the bill matures and the risk associated with it.

Loan For the purpose of temporarily transferring property (cash) from one party to another, a loan is an oral or written agreement between a lender and a borrower where the borrower agrees to return the property (cash) to the lender along with a predetermined interest rate.

Housing Finance: In the context of housing finance, a corporation provides financing for the purchase or construction of a house, as well as the purchase or development of land for that purpose.

Hire Purchase: Using a hire purchase system, a customer can buy things on credit and pay for them over time in instalments, with ownership of the products passing from seller to buyer upon completion of all payments.

Fee Based Services: Financial services that are based on a flat fee rather than commission are referred to as fee-based. The following services are classified as fee-based services:

Portfolio management: Manage and allocate funds on various known as portfolio alternatives known as portfolio management to lessen the unpredictability

Loan Syndication In loan syndication, many lenders pool their resources to lend money to a company or a project, and they share both the risk and the reward.

Foreign Collaboration: To put it another way, it is a joint effort of residents and non-residents to accomplish a common goal.

FINANCIAL REGULATORY AUTHORITIES

1. Securities and Exchange Board of India (SEBI)

A statutory organisation, (SEBI), was set up by the SEBI act of 1992 to combat market malpractices that eroded investor confidence. Preventing malpractice and guaranteeing appropriate and fair market functioning are its primary goals, as are protecting the interests of investors.

1. **Protective functions:** To defend the interests of the investors and other market participants. Preventing insider trading, educating investors, preventing price rigging, etc. are all part of it.
2. **Regulatory functions**: These are carried out in order to ensure the smooth operation of various market activities. Conducting an audit of exchanges, registering intermediaries .
3. **Development functions**: These activities are carried out with the goal of fostering the expansion of the financial markets. Training for intermediaries, research, supporting self-regulation, facilitating innovation, etc. are all part of it.

SEBI has the following powers

Abolish regulations governing how the stock market operates

To view the exchanges' records and financial statements.

To hold hearings and make decisions on cases of market malpractices.

Accept and impose delisting of businesses from stock exchanges. 4.

Participants who engage in misconduct will be subject to disciplinary measures such as fines and penalties.

For the purpose of regulating various intermediates and intermediaries such as brokers.

2. Reserve Bank of India (RBI)

It was created by the Reserve Bank of India Act of 1935 as India's central bank. The major role of the Reserve Bank of India (RBI) is to regulate and supervise the financial sector, particularly commercial banks and non-banking financial institutions. This institution is tasked with ensuring price and credit stability across the economy.

Functions of RBI are:

It was created by the Reserve Bank of India Act of 1935 as India's central bank. The major role of the Reserve Bank of India

(RBI) is to regulate and supervise the financial sector, particularly commercial banks and non-banking financial institutions. This institution is tasked with ensuring price and credit stability across the economy.

3. Insurance Regulatory and Development Authority of India (IRDAI)

Since 1999, India has had an independent, statutory organisation called the Insurance Regulator and Development Authority (IRDAI). Insurance policyholders' interests are protected, and the insurance business is developed and regulated. In order to keep insurance companies informed of any modifications to the laws and regulations, it regularly provides advisories.

Objectives of IRDA are:

- To ensure that the policyholder's interests are protected and treated fairly.
- To ensure the financial stability of the insurance industry by regulating the insurance companies.
- To avoid any uncertainty in the formulation of standards and rules.

Functions of IRDA are:

Insurance company registration can be granted, renewed, cancelled, or modified.

The IRDA statute mandates the collection of fees and charges.

Conducted a thorough inquiry into the operations of insurers and other insurance-related businesses.

Establishing a code of behaviour and offering training to intermediaries, insurance brokers, etc.

Protection of policyholder interests and a forum for resolution of grievances.

4. Pension Funds Regulatory and Development Authority (PFRDA)

Regulation and development of pension funds was given legal status with passage of the PFRDA Act in 2013. In India, it is the primary authority in charge of overseeing the pension industry. PFRDA initially only covered government employees, but its services were gradually expanded to all Indian citizens, including nonresident Indians (NRIs). Regulating pension funds and protecting subscribers' interests are the main goals of the Pension Fund Regulatory Authority (PFRA).

The PFRDA oversees the government's National Pension System (NPS). Custodians and trustee banks are also under its jurisdiction. CRA's of the PFRDA are responsible for maintaining pension fund records, accounting, and providing customer support to pension fund subscribers.

Functions of PFRDA are:

Investigating and questioning participants, mediators, and others.

Raising public knowledge of retirement savings and pension plans, as well as training intermediaries in these areas.

Disputes between pension fund subscribers and their intermediaries.

Regulating and registering third-party service providers.

Protection of pension fund beneficiaries' interests.

Specifying standards for pension fund investment.

For the pension business to have a code of conduct, standards of practise as well as terms and norms

5. Association of Mutual Funds in India (AMFI)

indian mutual funds association (amfi) was established in 1995 As a non-profit, self-regulatory organisation, it promotes the mutual fund business by enhancing professional and ethical standards, High ethical standards are implemented by AMFI to ensure that the mutual fund sector runs smoothly, which protects both investors as well as investment house owners alike. Investors and potential investors can see the Net Asset Value (NAV) of mutual funds on the AMFI's website every day. Searching for distributors of mutual funds has been made much easier as a result.

6. Ministry of Corporate Affairs (MCA)

MCA is a ministry of the Indian government that deals with corporate affairs. It is largely involved with the administration of the Companies Act, 1956, 2013 and other legislations, which governs the corporate sector. It lays out the norms and guidelines that must be followed in order for the corporate sector to operate legally.

UNIT-II
FINANCIAL MARKETS

Generally speaking, a financial market is not defined by a single region or location. Anyone who transacts money is considered to have done so in the financial markets, regardless of where it occurs. There are many different ways to go about raising capital, such as issuing stock or issuing loans from long-term lenders. You can also put money in a bank or buy debentures and then sell them. There are many different types of financial marketplaces, but they can all be described as places where people may purchase and sell various types of financial assets, claims, and services.

Markets for financial instruments, claims, or services are located at the heart of financial markets. People, businesses, and institutions all have access to the credit they need through it. It handles with a wide range of financial assets, including cash deposits, checks, bills, and bonds, amongst others. It is defined as a means of facilitating the movement of funds between investors and borrowers.

Shares, bonds, securities, and other financial instruments are traded in the financial market. It is possible for a financial market to exist in both a physical and virtual form (i.e., Internet).

A security's price rises or falls based on how much demand there is for it; if the demand is high, the price rises; otherwise, it falls.

In the financial world, the stock market serves as a conduit for transactions between buyers and sellers. Investment capital is mobilised on the financial markets from a variety of savings sources.

FUNCTION OF FINANCIAL MARKETS

1. **Borrowing and Lending**: One agent can transfer funds to another for investment or consumption objectives in the financial markets.
2. **Price Determination:** Price determination for freshly issued financial assets as well as the existing stock of financial assets is made possible through this mechanism.
3. **Information Aggregation and Coordination**: Data on financial asset valuations and the flow of money from lenders to borrowers is collected and aggregated by these organisations.
4. **Risk Sharing:** There is a risk transfer from those who invest to those that invest in those investments.
5. **Liquidity**: It allows those who own financial assets to sell or otherwise dispose of them.
6. **Efficiency**: Transaction and information expenses are reduced.

TYPES OF FINANCIAL MARKETS

1. Money Market: To put it another way, it's a short-term money market. It refers to the short-term borrowing and lending of funds by institutions. Short-term credit is available.

2. Capital Markets: A long-term securities market is what it is all about. It is recommended that the maturity period be at least four years lengthy. Financial instruments traded on the capital market are divided into three categories based on how long it will take them to mature: short-term, medium-term, and long-term. It is a long-term loan and borrowing market.

MONEY MARKET

It is the money market that deals with short-term financial instruments such as trade bills and promissory notes, as well as government papers drawn for less than one year. Short-term cash can be exchanged between lenders and borrowers through this system. It does not relate to a specific location where short-term funds are handled. All those involved in the exchange of short-term money are included. Liquidity or cash is provided to lenders while meeting the short-term needs of borrowers.

DEFINITIONS

There is a money market where short-term funds are loaned and repaid, where a major portion of the financial transactions of a country or the world are settled.

"The centre for dealing, generally of short term type, in monetary assets, it serves the short-term requirements of borrowers and delivers liquidity or cash to lenders."

FUNCTIONS OF MONEY MARKET

- The provision of short-term finance to industrial and other sectors helps economic development.
- It serves as a means of balancing the supply and demand of short-term capital.

It makes it easier for the RBI to carry out its monetary policy effectively.

- It offers a wide range of short-term investment options with reasonable returns.
- It helps commercial banks to become more financially disciplined.
- It is a short-term source of funding.
- It increases the creation of new capital by encouraging people to save and invest.
- Inter-banking transactions and money market instruments allow for short-term allocation of funds.
- It contributes to the creation of jobs.
- It helps the government deal with its budget shortfalls.
- It aids in inflation prevention.

In addition to deposits, it gives banks a reliable source of capital, opening the door to new types of financing and competition.

Furthermore, it increases competition for funds by encouraging the creation of non-bank intermediaries.

A wide variety of savings options are available to savers, allowing them to invest their resources.

COMPONENTS OF INDIAN MONEY MARKET

It is through the money market that an economy's short-term liquidity imbalances can be corrected. Thus, the growth and development of a country's economy is dependent on the development of its money market. The following are the most important elements of the Indian money market:

- **organized money market**: In these marketplaces, the rules, regulations, and processes that regulate the financial dealings are standardised. The government and Reserve Bank of India are responsible for regulating the country's organised money market. Banks, non-banking financial organisations and quasi-government bodies are all part of the Reserve Bank of India's money market.
- **unorganized money market**: indigenous bankers and money lenders are found in the unorganised sector, which is not regulated. Deposits are taken and loans are made. Non-banking companies, chit funds, and other types of private financing companies are also out there.
- **Sub market**: Call money market and bill market are the two components that make up this system. This market comprises of commercial and Treasury bills, certificates of deposits, and commercial papers.

CAPITAL MARKETS

The word "capital market" refers to the institutions that facilitate long-term financing. Private savings, both individual and corporate in nature, are translated into investments through fresh capital issues and also new public loans issued by government and semi-government agencies.

There are many different types of capital markets, but they all have one thing in common: they facilitate the transfer of money and financial resources from investors to entrepreneurs in the private and public sectors alike, regardless of whether they are private or public sector businesses.

Characteristics of Capital Market

- Long-term investment funds are available on the market.
- Makes it easier to borrow and lend money.
- Assists in capital rising.
- Requires the assistance of middlemen.

Marketable and not-for-marketable securities are both dealt with here.

Functions of Capital Market

1. Assists in the formation of capital.
2. Serve as a conduit between investors and savers.
3. It contributes to the country's economic growth.
4. Makes it easier to buy and sell.
5. Unproductive finances are diverted to more productive ones.
6. Reduces speculative behaviour.
7. Stabilizes the value of the stock market.
8. Boosts the economy.

PRIMARY MARKET

In the capital market, the primary market is a component. The selling of debt and equity-related securities allows the government, corporations, and other institutions to raise more funds. There are many different kinds of financial instruments that might be classified as primary market securities.

TYPES OF PRIMARY MARKET ISSUES

Public issue

It is one of the most prevalent means of distributing securities to the general population. In order to raise capital from various sources, the company goes public on the stock market. New investors can purchase these securities here. In this case, the new investor becomes a shareholder in the firm that is issuing the shares.

This is what we mean when we talk about an issue that affects the general public. Furthermore, the public concern is —

Initial Public Offer

An unlisted corporation is issuing new equity or convertible securities, as the name implies. In the past, these securities have been exchanged or made available for purchase to the general public. The company's stock is traded on the stock exchange after it has been listed. After a security is listed on the secondary market, an investor can purchase and sell it.

Further Public Offer or Follow on Offer or FPO.

When a publicly traded firm announces to the public that it will be issuing new shares. This is done by the publicly traded corporation in order to raise more money.

Rights issue

This is a different kind of problem that might occur in the main market. Existing shareholders are offered the opportunity to buy more shares in the company. The price at which securities are offered for sale is predetermined.

During a rights issue, investors can purchase shares at a discounted price for a predetermined time frame. It gives the company's current stockholders more power over the company's direction. It helps the company raise money without incurring additional expenses.

Bonus issue

An additional share of a corporation that has been fully paid for is given out to current shareholders at no cost. The company's free reserves or securities premium account are used to issue new shares. The company's present stockholders will get these shares as a bonus. Bonus shares, on the other hand, do not necessitate further funding.

Private placement

When a corporation makes its securities available to a small number of investors, it is referred to as a private placement. Bonds, stocks, and other financial instruments are all examples of securities. Individuals and institutions, as well as a combination of the two, may participate as investors.

Unlike an IPO, private placements are easier to raise. There are far less regulations in place. In addition, it saves money and time. Companies in their infancy can benefit from a private placement (like startups). An investment bank, a hedge fund, or an individual with an extremely high net worth can provide funds to the business (HNIs)

SECONDARY MARKET/STOCK EXCHANGE MARKET

The secondary market is where securities are sold to other investors. To put it another way, securities that have already passed through the new issue market can be traded here. For the most part, these securities are traded on the Stock Exchange, which provides a constant and regular market for trading. All stock exchanges recognised by the Government of India are included in this market. The Securities Contracts (Regulation) Act 1956 governs the Indian stock markets. It is the Bombay Stock Exchange, the country's primary stock market, that sets the tone for all other Indian stock exchanges.

The stock market would be incomplete without the presence of a stock exchange. In a secure environment, trade takes place in a systematic manner. Securities are purchased and sold here in accordance with clearly defined rules and guidelines. Debentures and shares issued by a publicly traded firm, as well as bonds and debentures issued by government agencies, municipalities, and other public entities, are all examples of securities that are discussed here.

FUNCTIONS/ROLE OF A STOCK EXCHANGE

Role of an Economic Barometer: As an economic barometer, the stock market serves as an indicator of the current state of the economy. Share price movements are logged in this chart. If you want to know what's going on in the world economy, you can look to this indicator.

Valuation of Securities: Supply and demand considerations are used to value stocks on the stock market. Stocks issued by companies with a strong track record of profitability and expansion are more highly valued. There are a number of benefits to valuing securities, including helping investors and creditors alike.

Transactional Safety: The securities that are traded on the stock market are listed, and the listing of securities is done only after checking the company's position. Transactional safety is maintained. To be included on the list, a company must follow the rules and regulations of the regulatory organisation.

Contributor to Economic Growth: A stock exchange is a place where investors can trade in the securities of a variety of different companies. As a result of the constant disinvestment and reinvestment that occurs in the trade process, new sources of capital are created and the economy as a whole grows.

Making the public aware of equity investment: To encourage consumers to invest in equity markets, stock exchanges release new issues and disseminate information about them.

Offers scope for speculation: A well-functioning stock market ensures that there is an adequate supply and demand for traded securities by allowing for reasonable speculation.

Facilitates liquidity: The primary function of the stock market is to facilitate the trading of securities. To put it another way, the stock market provides investors with the assurance that their current investments can be turned into cash.

Better Capital Allocation: In the equity market, companies that make money will have their stock exchanged frequently, allowing them to raise new capital. The stock market aids investors in properly allocating their capital in order to generate maximum profit.

Encourages investment and savings: The stock market is a major source of investment in numerous assets that can yield higher returns. 'It is better to invest in the stock market rather than gold and silver.

BOMBAY STOCK EXCHANGE

Dalal road in Mumbai is home to the Bombay Stock Exchange. At the end of December 2012, BSE was the eleventh-largest stock exchange in the world by market capitalisation, according to the NASDAQ Composite Index.

The BSE is India's oldest stock market. Some stock brokers gathered under a Banyan tree at the beginning of the year in 1855. However, as the number of stock representatives grew, the meeting was forced to relocate in 1874.

The Native Chor and Stock Brokers Affiliation was formed as an official organisation in 1875.

As early as 1986, the BSE created an index called the SENSEX to measure the performance of the trades executed. In the beginning, there existed a structure for exchanging open objections on the floor, but that was replaced by an electronic framework in 1995. Only fifty days after the trade, everything had changed.

In addition, the BSE provides a simple and efficient market for exchanging values, debentures and securities as well as other assets, such as subsidiaries and joint assets. It also provides an opportunity to trade the values of short and medium-term projects.

The Bombay Stock Exchange is home to almost 5000 companies. According to the BSE's market capitalization as of January 2013, the total value of all the companies listed is $1.32 trillion.

Administrations such as hazard management, settlement and cleaning are examples of these.

Automated systems and techniques are designed to keep the interest of financial professionals, revitalize markets worldwide and promote innovation. ISO 9000:2000 certification is the primary trade in India and the second-largest in the globe.

NATIONAL STOCK EXCHANGE

Mumbai is home to the National Stock Exchange. In 1992, it was consolidated, and by 1993, it had become a publicly traded corporation (IPO). The primary goal of this transaction was to increase transparency in financial transactions.

In June 1994, it began operating in the discount obligation advertise.

Since 1994, the National Stock Exchange's value-advertising portion has been in operation, while the subordinate portion has been in operation since 2000.

With over two million exchanging terminals, it offers a thoroughly modernised and completely mechanised screen-based exchanging framework that allows investors to trade from anywhere in India.

It has a crucial role to play in transforming the Indian value market to deliver more transparent, integrated, and efficient financial exchange.

It has a market value of more than $989 billion as of July 2013. The National Stock Exchange has records for 1635 different organisations.

Incredibly, financial experts all across India use the CNX NIFTY, the NSE's most popular stock index.

NSE was presented right away by driving Indian budgetary institutions. Among the services it provides are the ability to trade, repay, and settle debts, as well as the ability to do so through affiliates. As far as money, currency, and file trading goes, it's probably the biggest.

Numerous domestic and international businesses have an interest in the industry. GIC, LIC, SBI, and IDFC ltd. are all part of several household organisations.

The National Securities Depository Limited (NSDL) was also established by the NSE, which allowed investors to hold and manage their securities electronically through a demat account, as well.

Even one offer can be held and traded by a speculator. A physical treatment of safeguards is no longer necessary, as the risk of harm or loss of protections has fallen to a negligible level. India's securities market has become more accessible to both domestic and international investors thanks to the National Security Depository Constrainer's electronic security dealings, as well as the NSE's low exchange costs and high productivity in trading.

UNIT-III
MONEY MARKET

The Reserve Bank of India defines the 'Money Market' as a market for trading short-term financial assets. Assets like these can be used as a near equivalent for cash in the primary and secondary markets. So, the money market is essentially a mechanism that permits the lending and borrowing of short-term funds, which are typically of a year or less in duration. Among the characteristics of money market products are their short maturities and strong liquidity. The money market is made up of a variety of institutions, including commercial banks, nonbank financial companies (NBFCs), and acceptance houses.

Trade bills, government documents, promissory notes, and other financial instruments are used in money market transactions. Additionally, in order to conduct money market transactions, one must use formal paperwork, oral conversation, or written communication.

FEATURES OF MONEY MARKET INSTRUMENTS

1. High Liquidity

The high liquidity that these financial assets provide is one of their most important advantages. They provide a steady stream of income for the investor, and their short-term maturity makes them extremely liquid. Because of this, money market products are viewed as close substitutes for cash.

2. Secure Investment

Investing in these financial assets is one of the safest options on the market. Investing in money market instruments has a low probability of loss due to their issuers' excellent credit ratings and pre-determined returns.

3. Fixed returns

Investment returns are predetermined due to the fact that money market instruments are sold at a discount to their face value. This makes it easier for investors to pick the instrument that's right for them and their time horizon.

PURPOSE OF A MONEY MARKET

1. Maintains Liquidity in the Market

It is critical for the money market to preserve economic liquidity. The monetary policy framework includes a number of money market mechanisms. They are used by RBI to maintain a predetermined level of market liquidity.

2. Provides Funds at a Short Notice

Individuals, small and large businesses, and institutions can all borrow money quickly through the money market. These organisations are able to obtain short-term funding by selling money market instruments and borrowing money.

Institutions should borrow money from the market rather than banks since the method is simple and interest rates are lower than those on commercial loans, which are more expensive. Commercial banks have been known to make use of these money market instruments in order to meet the Reserve Bank of India's mandated minimum cash reserve ratio requirements.

3. Utilisation of Surplus Funds

There are a number of ways that investors can use the money market to get rid of excess funds while still keeping their liquidity intact. It makes it easier for people to put their money into the right kinds of investments. State and local governments as well as financial institutions are among these investors.

4. Aids in Financial Mobility

The Money Market facilitates financial mobility by facilitating the transfer of funds from one industry to the next. This ensures that the system is open and honest. By supporting industrial and commercial development, high financial mobility contributes to the general expansion of the economy.

5. Helps in monetary policy

The effective implementation of monetary policies is made possible by a well-developed money market. Short-term interest rates are a good indicator of the country's present monetary and banking situation because of money market transactions.

CALL MONEY MARKET

As part of the Indian Money Market, the day-to-day surplus funds of most banks are traded in the "call money market." "Call Money" refers to the money that is borrowed for a single day in this market.

One of the most important markets for short-term financial assets is known as the "money market." Liquidity and low costs are the most significant characteristics of a money market instrument, which allows lenders to balance their short-term surplus cash with the needs of borrowers.

Credit lines with a maturity of one to fourteen days are exchanged on the call money market. "Call Money" and "Notice Money" are the terms used to describe money that is lent for more than one day in this market, but less than 15 days. It's called "Term Money" when you borrow money from an interbank lending institution for at least 15 days.

MONEY MARKET INSTRUMENTS

Simply said, Money Market Instruments are anything that can be used to conduct business in the money market. In addition to allowing borrowers to meet their short-term needs, these products also provide lenders with convenient liquidity.

Treasury Bills (T-Bills)

Treasury Bills are one of the safest money market securities because they are issued by the government. Treasury bills, on the other hand, pose no risk. In other words, they carry no risk. As a result, their returns aren't very appealing. In the primary and secondary markets, Treasury bills are traded with maturities ranging from three months to one year. The government issues treasury bills at a lower price than their face value.

Certificate of Deposits (CDs)

As a deposit receipt, a Certificate of Deposit (CD) is issued by a financial institution or bank. A Certificate of Deposit, on the other hand, differs from a Fixed Deposit Receipt in at least two ways. There are two major differences between a CD and a regular bank account. Secondly, a Certificate of Deposit can be exchanged for any other asset. Certifcate of Deposits were first introduced by the RBI back in 1989 and have since become a popular alternative for short-term surplus investment .Another benefit for issuing banks is the high degree of liquidity associated with Certificates of Deposit. As an alternative, banks provide Certificates of Deposit that can be held for a period of up to 12 months. Individuals (excluding children), trusts, corporations, associations, funds, non-resident Indians, etc. are all eligible to receive them.

Commercial Papers (CPs)

Commercial Papers are unsecured short-term promissory notes issued by highly rated firms for the aim of raising funds from the market. In most cases, maturity periods range from one day to a maximum of 270 days for CPs. Commercial papers, popular in many nations promise bigger yields than Treasury Bills but are inherently less secure. There is a substantial secondary market for commercial papers.

Repurchase Agreements (Repo)

Short-term loans agreed upon by buyers and sellers for the purpose of selling and repurchasing are known as Repurchase Agreements (Repo), Reverse Repo, or simply Repo. Unless otherwise specified, only RBI-approved financial instruments including as treasury bills, government securities at the federal or state level, company debt, and PSU bonds may be exchanged.

Bankers Acceptance (BA)

A Bankers Acceptance (BA) is a document that promises future payment that is backed by a commercial bank. This form of remittance provides the details of the repayment, such as the amount due, the due date, and who is responsible for it, in a manner akin to a treasury bill. You can choose from 30- to 180-day maturities when using the Bankers Acceptance product.

COMMERCIAL BILL MARKET

There is a distinct difference between a commercial bill and a non-commercial bill. In the event when a customer purchases products on credit, the seller immediately issues a bill for the amount owed. It is immediately accepted by the buyer, who agrees to pay the stated sum by a given date. Self-liquidating paper and negotiable, a bill of exchange is prepared for a period of between three and six months.

CAPITAL MARKET

Funds for medium and long-term investments are traded in the capital market. All long- and medium-term funding sources are included under this umbrella group. Instruments and institutions that provide short-term financing are excluded (upto one year). Shares, debentures, bonds, funds, public deposits, etc. are the most common capital market instruments.

When investors put their money into a project, it's available to businesses and the government for use in the development of that initiative.

It acts as a conduit for organisations that have excess funds and are looking to transfer them to those in need of capital.

A variety of constructive uses are being made of these funds by the companies.

Functions of the Capital Market

Investors and savers are connected through the capital market.

It aids in the movement of capital to more productive locations in order to increase national GDP.

It increases economic output.

Savings can be used for long-term investment finance.

It makes it easier for investors to buy and sell shares.

It lowers the cost of transactions and the flow of information.

It is useful for quickly valuing financial assets.

Derivative trading provides protection against market volatility.

It facilitates the settling of transactions.

Capital allocation becomes more efficient.

There is a constant flow of funds available to businesses and the government.

INSTRUMENTS OF CAPITAL MARKET

1. Equities:

The term equity securities refer to the portion of a company's stock that is owned by its investors.

As a rule, equity holders are not paid on a monthly basis, but they can profit from capital gains if they decide to sell their stock.

In addition, equity holders receive ownership rights and join the ranks of corporate owners.

During a bankruptcy, equity holders are only entitled to a portion of the company's post-debt compensation.

As a part of their main business operations, many companies provide dividends to their shareholders on a regular basis.

2. Debt Securities:

Bonds and debentures are two types of debt securities.

1. Bonds:

Bonds are typically issued by the central and state governments, municipalities, and even corporations to finance infrastructure development or other types of projects.

The issuer of the bond is referred to as the borrower in this loaning capital market transaction.

Fixed-term bonds are those that have a predetermined duration after which they must be surrendered. As a result, when the bonds reach maturity, the issuers are required to pay back the principal to the bondholders.

2. Debentures:

In contrast to bonds, which are backed by collateral, debentures are unencumbered investment choices.

In this case, investors become prospective creditors of the issuing institution or firm.

3. Derivatives:

Assets such as currency, bonds, stocks, and stock indexes are used as the underlying assets for derivative instruments in the capital markets.

Forwards, futures, options, and interest rate swaps are the most prevalent types of derivative securities.

- **Forward:** When two parties agree to exchange something at a predetermined price, it is known as a forward contract.
- **Future:** It is possible to trade futures at a predetermined price on a predetermined date in the future, which is known as a derivative.
- **Options:** Derivatives options are contracts in which two parties agree to buy or sell a specific quantity of derivatives at a specific price for a specific length of time, known as an option.

4. Exchange-Traded Funds:

The financial resources of numerous investors are pooled in exchange-traded funds, which are then used to purchase a variety of capital market items, such as stocks, bonds, and derivatives.

SEBI-registered exchange-traded funds make it an appealing alternative for investors with only a basic understanding of the Indian stock market.

Shares in ETFs that have characteristics of both stocks and mutual funds are traded in the stock market in blocks.

In the course of normal equities trading, investors can buy and sell ETF funds listed on stock exchanges.

UNIT-IV

FINANCIAL INSTITUTION

Savings and investment in productive activities are facilitated by financial organisations such as insurance firms. In return, they guarantee the safety of investors' lives or assets in the event of an emergency. That is to say, they take on their own the risk of a customer's loss.

Most financial institutions fall into the following categories: central banks; retail banks; internet banks; credit union etc.

In a country, financial institutions, also known as financial intermediaries, play an important role in the financial system. They are primarily responsible for raising money and ensuring that it gets to the people who need it.

ROLE OF FINANCIAL INSTITUTIONS

For those who have more money than they need, financial institutions serve as a conduit for the transfer of that money into a more productive use. There are numerous ways in which these institutions contribute to the growth of the economy.

1. Providing funds: They assist a significant number of people in pursuing a career in the industrial sector. Economic growth can be accelerated by the construction of new industrial facilities and the expansion of existing ones. There are a lot of funds available for investment at financial institutions.

2. Infrastructural facilities: Institutions of finance plan their investment strategies with a focus on national interests. In order to assist the country grow, the institutions invest in the areas that can.

3. Promotional activities: Starting a new business unit is something that financial institutions can do because they have the know-how and staff to do it. Because of this, these organisations step up to help small business owners. Increasing a country's development is made easier by financial institutions' promotional efforts.

4. Development of backward areas: The establishment of new businesses in underdeveloped areas is aided by financial institutions that give particular assistance for entrepreneurs. Many of India's leading financial institutions prefer financing to businesses located in economically depressed areas and demand lower rates of interest. Entrepreneurs will be encouraged to set up new businesses in underdeveloped areas as a result of these efforts.

5. Planned development: Different institutions have designated their areas of expertise so that all businesses can benefit. It is important to note that some financial institutions like SIDBI and SFCI support small businesses while others like IFCI and SIDC lend money to major businesses. Foreign trade, tourism, and other sectors rely on the assistance of many institutions.

6. Accelerating industrialization: Direct and indirect jobs will be generated, commodities and services will be made available, and the level of living will rise as a result. Financial institutions assist emerging businesses by providing financial, managerial, and technical assistance.

7. Employment generation: There are numerous people working at the company's offices. Additionally, financial specialists are needed to assist in the financing of lending offers. In addition, they encourage the establishment of businesses in underdeveloped areas, which creates jobs.

DEVELOPMENT BANKS

Investments in infrastructure, mining, heavy industry, and irrigation systems, all of which need substantial upfront capital but have long-term return periods, are typically financed by development banks (DFIs). It sets the groundwork for the country's future industrial development. Agriculture development banks like NABARD can be found all over the world.

Others call development banks "term lending institutions" or "development finance institutions (DFI)".

FEATURES OF DEVELOPMENT BANK

Financing for businesses in the medium and long term is provided by this sort of financial organization.

For one thing, it does not accept public money.

Short-term loans aren't the only thing this bank does. It is a multifaceted financial institution.

In its most basic form, it is a bank for economic growth. Its principal objective is to encourage investment and entrepreneurship in developing economies. It encourages the growth of small and medium-sized businesses and seeks a more balanced regional development.

Furthermore, it gives financial aid to both private and public-sector businesses.

Traditional financial channels, such as those provided by banks and other conventional lenders, are unaffected. As a gap-filler, it fills in the holes left by other financial instruments. Instead of making money, it aims to serve the public interest. As a whole, it is beneficial to the country.

OBJECTIVES OF DEVELOPMENT BANK

Increased job prospects, increased exports, and a rise in import substitution are all reasons to favour industrial growth in regressive areas.

Encourage more self-employment initiatives; resuscitate ailing units;

Improve large-industry management;

Eliminate regional discrepancies or imbalances;

Support growth of science and technology in new sectors by providing risk capital; strengthen the country's capital market;

COMMERCIAL BANKS

It is a commercial bank that accepts deposits from the general public and lends money to businesses in order to generate profits.

When it comes down to it, commercial banks are profit-seeking institutions in the truest sense of the word.

They typically use short-term loans to fund trade and commerce. As a result, the banks make their money from the difference between the interest rates they charge their borrowers and the rate they pay their depositors, which results in a large profit margin.

FUNCTIONS OF COMMERCIAL BANK

Primary Functions

Accepting Deposits – Savings, fixed, and current deposits are all forms of deposits accepted by commercial banks.

Savings Deposits – A customer can deposit money into their account up to a predetermined amount. Individuals on a fixed income tend to like these types of accounts since they allow them to accumulate savings over time.

Fixed Deposits – Lock-in periods for fixed deposits are typically three to six months.

Current Deposits – Account holders can make deposits and withdrawals at any time using a current deposit. Overdrafts are available to individuals and corporations in various current accounts up to a predetermined maximum.

Providing Loans – Commercial banks play a major role in the economy by lending money to businesses and individuals and profiting from the interest they generate. Typically, banks keep a modest amount of money in reserve to cover their costs, while offering customers a variety of short- and long-term loans.

Credit Creation – Commercial banks have a unique ability to create credit. When a corporation or commercial entity needs a lump sum of money right away, a bank will issue a line of credit and then transfer the funds to that entity all at once.

Secondary Functions

Providing locker Facilities – Customers who wish to store valuables in a secure location can do so at commercial banks. When left unattended, personal belongings in a locker are vulnerable to theft or damage.

Dealing in Foreign Exchange – Individuals and businesses who export or import items from abroad rely on commercial banks to assist them get foreign currency. There are a limited number of financial institutions authorised to carry out foreign currency transactions, however.

Exchange of Securities Commercial banks also deal in bonds and other types of securities. It is more convenient for customers to buy or sell the units directly from the financial institution, rather than through an intermediary.

Discounting Bills of Exchange – Today, the primary function of a commercial bank is to discount commercial customers' bills. Banks perceive bill discounting to be a beneficial investment. As a negotiable instrument, bills ensure a consistent inflow of funds while posing no financial risk during payment. They also don't involve any kind of legal action on the part of the financial institution.

Bank as an Agent – As an agent, a commercial bank is also required to provide financial services to its customers. For the most part, these companies provide: Acting as a trustee, executor or administrator of a customer's estate.

Assisting with the processing of cheques, draughts, bills, and other forms of electronic payment.

PUBLIC SECTOR BANKS

In our country, public sector banks are financial institutions in which the central government holds a majority share, which should be more than 50%. Core banking, made possible by technological advancements, was implemented in the country and has since extended to every nook and cranny.

In our country, public sector banks are financial institutions in which the central government holds a majority share, which should be more than 50%. Currently, there are 27 public sector banks in the country, including 21 nationalised banks and six State Bank Group banks, as well as their five associates. With the nationalizations of IDBI in 2011 and of Bharatiya Mahila Bank in 2014, we've now reached a new height. People all around the country rely on these institutions for all of their banking needs. A major reason for nationalising bank ownership and control in the country was to remove it from private hands and shatter the power of the country's most powerful and wealthy families. Because of this, money and economic power were not concentrated in a few hands. Furthermore, it became a significant organisation because it tapped into the savings of people across the country, allowing them to form a single string across the entire nation. As a result of global economic expansion and other circumstances, public sector banks have exhibited amazing business since 2002-03, and their profit has continued to expand since then.

FUNCTIONS OF PUBLIC SECTOR BANKS

The country's public banking system has come a long way since its foundation. Core banking, made possible by technological advancements, was implemented in the country and has since extended to every nook and cranny. Customers and bank personnel alike appreciate how much easier their lives have become as a result of it. Public and private sector banks both perform the same basic function: mobilising resources and capitals amassed via various deposits and schemes over a variety of time periods and lending them out to their own clients at higher interest rates in order to increase their own profits. In addition, the bank offers services such as lockers, remittance, draught generation, check collection and transfer, and bank guarantee credit to its customers. Insurance and mutual funds are also available to its customers in addition to loan options and the opportunity to save their money.

PRIVATE SECTOR BANKS

They are excellent service providers since they operate in a more competitive and converse environment in India. They provide a wider range of services and products than the government-owned banks. They protect the confidentiality and safety of their clients' personal information.

IMPORTANCE OF PRIVATE SECTOR BANKS

(i) Offering high degree of Professional Management:

Professional management and marketing concepts are introduced into banking by private sector banks. As a result, the public sector banks are able to acquire the same expertise and technological resources.

(ii) Creates healthy competition:

The competition among the private sector banks keeps the banking system's efficiency at a high level.

(iii) Encourages Foreign Investment:

Foreign investment in the country is heavily influenced by private sector banks, particularly foreign banks.

(iv) Helps to access foreign capital markets:

Financial assistance from the international capital markets is provided by private sector foreign banks to Indian firms and government organisations. Because of the presence of their headquarters and other branches in major foreign cities, this service is made simpler for them. As a result, they play a significant role in promoting the country's trade and industry.

(v) Helps to develop innovation and achieve expertise:

As a result, private sector banks are constantly working to develop new product outlets (new schemes, services, etc.) and help their clients become experts in their respective industries.

NEW GENERATION BANK

To be termed a new generation bank, a bank must have an innovative strategy that attracts new clients, rather than a marketing strategy that merely serves to bring in new customers in the short term.

In India, there are seven banks of the "new generation" generation. Axis Bank, Development Credit Bank, HDFC Bank, ICICI Bank, Indusind Bank, Kotak Mahindra Bank, and Yes Bank are the names of these institutions.

EXIM BANK

The Export-Import Bank of India, or EXIM Bank, is India's major export financing institution that works to integrate foreign commerce and investment with the country's economic progress. It was established by the Indian Government in 1982 and is a wholly-owned subsidiary. David Rasquinha is the company's current chief executive officer. A Mumbai, Maharashtra-based organisation.

EXIM BANK FUNCTIONS

Financial Products

- **Buyer's credit** Exporters in India are encouraged to explore new markets around the world through this financial facility scheme. Exports for small and medium-sized enterprises (SMEs) are also facilitated by providing international purchasers with financing to purchase Indian goods.
- **Corporate banking** – Export-oriented Indian enterprises might benefit from a variety of financing options offered by the government.
- **Lines of credit** – As an effective market-entry tool, it extends a line of credit to Indian exporters in order to assist them expand into new markets.
- **Project exports** It promotes the export of Indian projects and aids Indian firms in obtaining contracts overseas.

Services

- **Marketing advisory services** – To aid in the globalisation of Indian exporters by helping them locate abroad distributors and partners. Helps to find prospects for plant projects and acquisitions abroad.
- **Research and analysis** – does economic and investment research on a global scale to uncover potential dangers.
- **Export advisory services** There is a wide range of services available to help exporters assess international risks and opportunities and maximize their competitiveness.

INSURANCE COMPANIES

Direct insurance or reinsurance services are offered by financial intermediaries such as insurance companies, which provide financial protection against potential risks in the future.

FUNCTIONS OF AN INSURANCE COMPANY

1] Provides Reliability

An insurance policy's primary purpose is to protect against the possibility of a sudden and unanticipated financial loss. This is a major source of concern for any company. With this uncertainty, it provides monthly payment (the premium) as the guarantee of regularity.

2] Protection

Insurance does not lessen the risk of a company's losses or damages. Such a loss, however, is guarded against by this measure. In this way, the organisation is spared the kind of financial harm that would cripple its day-to-day operations.

3] Pooling of Risk

All policyholders in an insurance company combine their risks. If one of them has a financial setback, the reward will come from this pool of pre-tax dollars they've all paid into. As a result, everyone of them has some of the responsibility for the outcome of the situation.

4] Legal Requirements

In many circumstances, insurance is really mandated by the law of the land. For example, if you're transporting goods, or if you're opening a public location, you may be required to have fire insurance. We will be able to meet these stipulations with the assistance of an insurance business.

5] Capital Formation

The insurance company's capital is derived in part from the collective premiums of its customers. The corporation can then use this money to fund productive investments that pay off in the form of revenue.

NBFCS

A non-banking financial institution is one that accepts deposits in any form, whether they are made in one lump sum or in instalments through donations or some other means (Residuary non-banking company).

Non-bank financial institutions (NBFCs) provide a range of services, including lending and other lending-related operations such as advance lending.

Before participating in any NBFC activities, you must first register with the NBFC.

Hire, lease, infrastructure, investment, venture capital and housing financing are just some of the services they provide.

In order to take a deposit from a customer, NBFCs only accept term deposits and deposits that can be withdrawn at any time.

NBFC – SIGNIFICANCE

Many people and enterprises in developing nations, such as India, are unable to obtain bank loans because of the high cost of borrowing.

Due to the fundamental characteristics of nonbanking financial institutions, such as NBFCs in India, they provide services to market segments that commercial banks do not serve because of higher risk and lower returns.

UNIT-V

FINANCIAL SERVICES

Products and services given by financial institutions to facilitate various financial transactions and other associated activities are referred to as financial services financial intermediation is another name for financial services.

Financial services encompass a wide range of operations, including banking, investing, and insurance. Financial products, on the other hand, are the real items, accounts, or investments that financial services organisations and their professionals offer.

FINANCIAL SERVICES INDUSTRY

With the broad definition of "financial services," it's easy to see that this industry's diverse products include everything from insurance and money management to payments and digital banking.

In the world of financial services, there are many players and moving elements, including credit card issuers, processors, and legacy banks.

SCOPE OF FINANCIAL SERVICES

Since it includes so many different services, this is the case. Financial services can be divided into two broad categories:

A. ASSET/FUND BASED SERVICES

An asset or money acquisition service is one that is employed by a consumer. Companies can get working capital and long-term loans through asset-based lending, which uses assets like accounts receivable, inventories, machinery, equipment, and real estate as security. A loan to a business that is backed by a piece of the business's property is what we mean by this term.

1. Equipment leasing/Lease financing:

In a lease, a company receives the right to use a capital asset like machinery or other equipment for a charge known as lease rentals, which are agreed upon in advance. The lessee is the person or organisation that receives the right to use the property. The asset does not become his to keep. Only the right to use the item is transferred to him. The lessor is the individual (or company) who grants the permission.

2. Hire purchase and consumer credit:

Hire buy is a viable alternative to leasing a product. Hiring purchase is a transaction in which things are purchased and sold on the condition that payment is made over a predetermined amount of time. Only the commodities themselves are transferred to the buyer. I have nothing to do with it. After he pays the final installment, he is entitled to possession. The seller has the right to take back the products if the buyer doesn't make any payments. Interest is paid on each of the payments.

3. Bill discounting:

Finance companies offer bill discounting as a fund-based financial solution. The bearer of a time bill does not have to wait until the bill's due date to pay it. The bill can be discounted with his banker if he is short on cash. When a banker subtracts a specified amount (discount), they credit the customer's account with the net amount. As a result, the bank buys the bill and deducts the discounted amount from the customer's account. The banker receives money from the drawee on the due day. If he doesn't pay, the bank will get the money back from the person who discounted the bill. When it comes to discounting of bills, lending money against a bill of exchange is referred to as "discounting."

4. Venture capital:

Simply put, venture capital refers to money that can be used to start a business from scratch. It entails lending money to small and medium-sized businesses. An extremely high rate of return is sought by investing in a high-risk enterprise. The phrase "venture capital" refers to both short-term risk capital as well as long-term equity funding.

5. Insurance services:

When two people agree to insure each other, they've entered into an agreement called an insurance contract. The insured and the insurer are one and the same. The individual whose life or property is covered by an insurance policy is referred to as the "insured." Insurers, on the other hand, refer to those who have taken out insurance policies. The insurer is the company to which the insured transfers risk. Insurer, on the other hand, refers to the person who covers the risk of the insured. As a result, insurance is a legal agreement between the parties involved. For a fee, the insurance company promises to reimburse the insured should a certain event occur, such as the death of a loved one. If you lose money due to a risk you're covered for by insurance, you'll get your money back from your insurance company.

6. Factoring:

Account receivables (arising from credit sales of products or services) are purchased by the factor and immediately paid to the supplier by the factor. A financial institution or banker buys the accounts receivables of a company (client) in this arrangement. Consequently, the factor provides financing to the client (supply) in the form of account receivables to the factor. Account receivables are collected on behalf of the factor. In this case, the financial institution (factor) assumes the risk. The factor charges a fee for this type of service as well as for the interest. Factor age is the name given to this tax or levy.

1. Forfeiting:

Forfeiting is a method of financing international trade receivables. Export receivables purchased by a bank or other financial institution are non-recourse purchases. When supplying products to a buyer, the exporter relinquishes his right to claim future payment from that buyer to the forfeiter. Using forfeiting, an exporter can sell his goods on credit while still receiving the money in advance. In a nutshell, forfeiting is the practise of a forfeiter (finance agency) discounting an export bill and paying the exporter in cash. Getting paid for exports isn't a concern for the exporter at all. For the time being, he can focus solely on exports.

2. Mutual fund:

Investing in corporate and government assets is the primary function of mutual funds, which act as middlemen between investors and their money. In addition to the dividends, interest, and capital gains, mutual fund managers profit from actively managing this stock portfolio. In the end, mutual fund shareholders receive the profits.

NON-FUND BASED/FEE BASED FINANCIAL SERVICES

The public sector banks' non-fund financial services include loan syndication, consultation, and so on.

1. Merchant banking

In essence, merchant banking is a form of service banking that focuses on arranging funds rather than actually giving them. An middleman is everything that the commercial banker does. Its primary function is to move money from those who have it to others who require it. With today's modern-day merchant banker, financial institutions, banks, stock markets, as well as money markets are all able to comprehend each other. According to SEBI (Merchant Bankers) Rule, 1992, "any person involved in issue management either by arranging arrangements for selling, buying, or subscribing to securities" is a "merchant banker" as defined by the SEBI (Merchant Bankers) Rule.

2. Credit rating

A credit rating is an assessment of a company's willingness and ability to satisfy its financial obligations on time and in full by a third-party rating agency. It assesses the issuer's ability and willingness to repay both interest and principal over the term of the rated instrument.. It's an assessment of the financial and commercial prospects of a company. In a nutshell, a credit rating is an assessment of a company's creditworthiness by a third party.

3. Stock broking:

Brokerage is now being used as a professional service for investment advice. Any member of a recognised stock exchange qualifies as a stock broker. Is he involved in the purchase or sale of securities (shares)? To become a stock broker, one must be registered with the Securities and Exchange Board of India (SEBI). There are rules, regulations, and bylaws to follow as a stock exchange member.

4. Securitisation (of debt):

The bank's loans to clients are valuable assets. Loan assets are what you'd name them. Loan assets, in contrast to investment assets, cannot be traded or transferred. As a result, loan assets aren't readily available for use in other financial transactions. The issue here is how to make a bank's loan more readily available. The solution to this issue is to convert the loans into tradable securities. Loans can now be repaid in full. They acquire the quality of being marketable. Securitization is used to accomplish this. As a new method of securing loans, securitization has gained popularity. Investors can purchase marketable securities, which are created via the transformation of current or anticipated cash flows. As a result, any asset that may be securitized can be. An illiquid asset is turned into a security that can be traded on the open market later on through the process of "securitization". Simplified, securitization is the process of turning non-liquid and untradeable asset classes into securities that can be traded on the open markets. The procedure by which the assets of a lending institution are converted into tradable securities. Factoring and securitization are not the same. Transferring debts without changing them into marketable securities is called factoring. Securitization, on the other hand, necessitates the conversion of illiquid assets into marketable securities.

DEBIT CARD

Using a debit card, you can make purchases using money you've already deposited at the bank. Using a debit card means that a consumer's checking account will be debited when the card is used. In addition to purchasing products or services, these cards can also be used to withdraw cash from an ATM or from a merchant who will allow you to add an additional amount to a purchase. They are also known as "check cards" or "bank cards."

Fast, simple, and convenient transactions are made possible by debit cards. Cash can be provided to you through the use of a debit card. It is possible to withdraw money from an ATM with these cards. As a result, it serves as a reserve for unexpected expenses.

CREDIT CARD

Using a credit card, you can make purchases online without having to pay with cash. The number on each card is unique. It is possible to buy products or services by using this number, together with additional information on the card (such as the expiration date or a code). The money is then transferred to the seller by the card's issuer.

Paying for purchases later is possible with a credit card. This is similar to a short-term loan in that regard. To a certain extent, you are making a purchase using the money of the credit card company.

In terms of security, credit cards are better than debit cards because they are less likely to be stolen. You don't have to alter your spending habits to reap the benefits. Monitoring your spending is a lot simpler now. One of the quickest and easiest ways to establish credit is to utilise a credit card wisely.

INSURANCE PRODUCTS

Insurance Products include any insurance, indemnity, annuity, or similar product by which one agrees to pay or provide a certain sum or determinable benefit or annuity in connection with certain specified scenarios.

Financial uncertainty and unintended loss are the primary goals of this policy. There are many ways to achieve this, but the most common is by paying a modest, known fee—an insurance premium—to an insurance company in exchange for an agreement to pay out in the case of a huge loss.

FINANCIAL SECTOR REFORMS

Reforms in the financial sector often include the liberalisation of interest rates, the liberalisation of quantitative constraints, such as credit and exchange controls, and steps to improve the allocation efficiency and soundness of the financial sector, notably the banking sector.

RBI AND SEBI GUIDELINES TO FINANCIAL MARKETS AND SERVICES

After receiving feedback from SEBI, banks, and other stakeholders, the Reserve Bank of India (RBI) decided to implement some changes. Among the amendment's provisions is the prohibition on any bank from:

- Under no circumstances may a deposit-taking non-banking finance company or NBFC own more than 10% of the equity of the organisation.
- If you want to invest more than 10% of a Real Estate Investment or Infrastructure Investment Trust's unit capital, you must stay within the 20% net worth limit for investments in stocks, convertible bonds/debentures, equity-oriented

mutual funds, and exposure to Alternative Investment Funds (AIFs)

- More than 20 percent of the paid-up share capital of the investment firm operating in non-financial services may be held by subsidiaries, affiliates, joint ventures, or entities directly or indirectly controlled by the bank.
- You must invest at least one dollar in a Category III AIF. Investing in a Category III AIF by a bank's subsidiary must be limited to the SEBI's regulatory minimums.
- A second part of the amendment mandates that banks conduct an internal capital adequacy assessment (ICAAP) to identify any risks associated with equity investments in Alternative Investment Funds (AIFs) that they make directly or indirectly through their subsidiaries, and that they determine the necessary additional capital as part of the SREP. Similarly, banks supporting Infrastructure Debt Funds would be held to the same standards. According to the proposed amendment, "it [bank] has the minimum mandated capital (including Capital Conservation Buffer) following investment" will now read "it [bank] has."
- To sell mutual funds, the company must be a separate AMC. A parent company or AMC must have a minimum net value of Rs 50,000,000. The Reserve Bank of India (RBI) is required to register money market mutual funds, whereas SEBI is required to register all other mutual funds.

REFERENCES

1. Financial Markets And Services by Gordan (Author)
2. Financial Markets & Services – Dr. L. Natarajan
3. Financial Markets Institutions & Services By Jagroop Singh (Author)
4. Financial Markets Institutions and Services by Sandeep Goel (Author)
5. Financial Markets, Institutions & Financial Services by Prof. Bimal Jaiswal (Author), Dr. Bhuvana Venkatraman (Author), & 1 Mor

www.ingramcontent.com/pod-product-compliance
Lightning Source LLC
LaVergne TN
LVHW020011170826
845677LV00022B/2637

* 9 7 8 9 3 9 3 2 3 9 0 0 6 *